PRESBYTERIAN CHURCH (U.S.A.)
OFFICE OF THE GENERAL ASSEMBLY

MW01254855

Dear Fri

As n

ground in.

better way to reclaim that common ground than ___ ___
emphasis on "The Great Ends of the Church." They are what
unite Presbyterians and set our direction for mission.

The Great Ends of the Church are a real jewel. They were
developed in the former United Presbyterian Church of
North America as that church faced a new century in the
early 1900s. As we begin a new millennium, it is critical that
we also reflect on those things that are central to our calling
and our life together.

We find The Great Ends of the Church in the first
chapter of our *Book of Order* (G–1.0200):

> The great ends of the church are the proclamation of
> the gospel for the salvation of humankind; the shelter,
> nurture, and spiritual fellowship of the children of God;
> the maintenance of divine worship; the preservation of
> the truth; the promotion of social righteousness; and the
> exhibition of the Kingdom of Heaven to the world.

What a wonderful vision. The great ends make it clear
that our common calling is an inclusive one. The call to
share the gospel is matched by a commitment to social
justice. The need for a renewal in worship is matched by a
commitment to truth. The imperative of building up the
Christian community is matched by a call to exhibit the
Kingdom of Heaven to all the world.

The 209th General Assembly (1997) called on Presbyterian
churches, governing bodies, and institutions to reshape their
lives in line with the great ends of the church. This resource
helps us understand this vision more clearly and offers ways
for congregations to move toward these great ends.

Clifton Kirkpatrick
Stated Clerk of the General Assembly

Worship Resources Recalling the Six "Great Ends of the Church"

Introduction

In 1910, the United Presbyterian Church in North America (UPNA) formally adopted a set of missional statements that was intended to define its life and work. Called the "Six Great Ends of the Church," these brief phrases attempted to draw together elements of belief and practice that could be traced through our confessional history to the very teachings of Jesus himself as they are recorded in the Gospels.

Nine decades and two denominational mergers later, these statements remain in the Constitution of the Presbyterian Church (U.S.A.), and they appear in the opening pages of the *Book of Order*:

> The great ends of the church are the proclamation of the
> gospel for the salvation of humankind; the shelter,
> nurture, and spiritual fellowship of the children of God; the
> maintenance of divine worship; the preservation of the
> truth; the promotion of social righteousness; and the
> exhibition of the Kingdom of Heaven to the world.
>
> *Book of Order* (G-1.0200)

Because these six Great Ends offer a way of informing our life and witness as Presbyterians, it seems both appropriate and desirable to create and collect worship materials that recognize the Great Ends in intentional ways as the people of God gather at the Font, the Pulpit, and the Table. From the gathering around these identity-giving centers, the church goes out into the home, the workplace, and the world, empowered to live a sacramental life (W-7.1002).

This resource is designed to encourage and assist congregations, presbyteries, synods, and other entities throughout the church to lift the Great Ends in worship. The ideas and the liturgies that follow present both the text and the spirit of the six Great Ends for use in a variety of settings. Each of the larger liturgies begins with a quotation drawn from our confessional heritage, the *Book of Confessions*. Each, then, presents the focus of one of the Great Ends in the context of the Service for the Lord's Day, Daily Prayer, or a Festival of Readings and Music. In keeping with our theology and the Directory for Worship in the *Book of Order*, the celebration of the Eucharist is anticipated as the normative practice for the Lord's Day (W-2.4009).

These materials, both text and illustrations, may be reproduced as they appear, or they may offer worship planners ideas, designs, and resources on which to draw for use in contextually specific settings. Citations in the text refer to the most current publications of the Presbyterian Church (U.S.A.).

It is our hope that worship planners throughout the church will lift the Great Ends as an expression of our common faith and calling. May God be glorified and Christ be made known in and through all we say and do.

The Great Ends and Worship: Possibilities

The six "Great Ends of the Church" reflect the affirmation made in the beginning sentence of the Directory for Worship: "The life of the Church is one . . . its worship, witness, and service are inseparable." The Directory goes on to say, "Christian worship joyfully ascribes all praise and honor, glory and power to the triune God. . . . In worship the faithful offer themselves to God and are equipped for God's service in the world" (W-1.1000).

Worship planners face the challenge of providing liturgy through which the faithful may hear and respond to God's Word, renew their identity, and meet the risen Christ again and again as they participate in the Sacraments. From these encounters with God in worship, the people go out to serve and become doers of God's Word through service in the world. While it is true that the six Great Ends were conceived and crafted by people of a different time and place, it is also true that all six of these statements share the core conviction that the Christian life, in any time and in any situation, is lived in joyful praise and in faithful response to the call of Christ. Understood in light of the issues and challenges facing this generation, these same texts can provide inspiration and guidance for the living of these, the closing days of the twentieth century.

Lectionary

Just as the *Book of Common Worship* ". . . seeks to rise above sectarian limitations in embodying the prayer of the church ecumenical" (*BCW*, p. 7), so the worship life of Presbyterian congregations should express both the fullness of Reformed tradition and the worship language and form that is common to various portions of the body of Christ. In this time of ecumenical convergence and new understandings of liturgy as theology, such a foundation is imperative for our common worship life. One of the ways we engage in *common* worship is through the use of the lectionary common to various parts of the body of Christ.

The Revised Common Lectionary, used extensively throughout the English-speaking church, provides structure and continuity for the reading and interpretation of Scripture. In congregations where the Lectionary is used, worship planners may wish to weave themes of the six Great Ends into the fabric of the Service for the Lord's Day at the times and seasons when such emphases would be particularly appropriate. For example, the phrase *"The proclamation of the gospel for the salvation of humankind"* may be incorporated easily into the lectionary readings for the seasons of Advent, Christmas, Epiphany, Lent, and Easter, when the church ponders the life, ministry, death, and resurrection of Jesus Christ. The phrase *"the exhibition of the Kingdom of Heaven to the world"* could be used during the Pentecost season, fitting with the lectionary readings for that time in the life of the worshiping community.

Headings for the Movement of Worship

The Service for the Lord's Day, as it appears in the *Book of Common Worship*, is divided into an historic fourfold order: Gathering, The Word, The Eucharist, and Sending. In lifting the Great Ends through the liturgy, the headings of each of the various portions of any Lord's Day service could be amplified to read as follows:

GATHERING:
Attending to the Maintenance of Divine Worship

THE WORD:
Attending to the Proclamation of the Gospel
for the Salvation of Humankind

THE EUCHARIST:
Attending to the Shelter, Nurture, and Spiritual
Fellowship of the Children of God

SENDING:
Attending to the Exhibition of the
Kingdom of Heaven to the World

Acts of Worship

The arrangement of the Service for the Lord's Day might include the identification of specific acts of worship as fulfillment of the Great Ends of the Church. The Affirmation of Faith might be seen as a means for the "Preservation of the Truth," preceding the creed, confessional statement, or portions of such documents as A Brief Statement of Faith of the Presbyterian Church (U.S.A.) with these introductory words:

> God calls the Church to affirm what it believes; in that affirmation, we seek to work for [the preservation of the truth]. Let us confess our faith:

The entire Great Ends statement (*Book of Order,* G-1.0200), could also be adapted for use as the Affirmation of Faith for the day.

Prayers, including forms and texts suggested in the *Book of Common Worship,* may be modified to reflect the Great Ends of the Church. Examples of this idea include the following:

Prayer of the Day   *BCW*, p. 51, no. 2

". . . may be joined with all your works
in praising you for your great glory.
[Empower your people here gathered
to fulfill the calling of Jesus Christ
and to worship and live
so that the great ends of the Church are fulfilled
in this community of faith and beyond]."

Prayer of Confession   *BCW*, p. 54, no. 3

". . . and passed by the hungry, the poor, and the oppressed,
[failing to heed your example
and your calling to the church of Jesus Christ
to work for the promotion of social righteousness
and the exhibition of the Kingdom of Heaven to the world]."

Baptism: Presentation   *BCW*, p. 403

"[In baptism, God calls the Church
to the proclamation of the gospel for the salvation of humankind,
and the shelter, nurture and fellowship of the children of God.]
Hear the words of our Lord Jesus Christ:. . . ."

It is appropriate to insert prayers of intercession that lift up phrases of the six Great Ends, as for example:

Eucharist: Great Prayer of Thanksgiving   *BCW*, pp. 72ff

"Remember your church. . . .
Unite it in the truth of your Word
and [in the preservation of the truth.
Equip your saints for the proclamation of the gospel
for the salvation of humankind.]
Remember the world of nations. . . .
By your Spirit renew the face of the earth;
[lead your church in the promotion of social
righteousness and the exhibition of the Kingdom of
heaven to the world, and] let peace and justice prevail.
Remember our family and friends. . . .
[Give us a spirit of faithfulness in the shelter, nurture,
and fellowship of the children of God.]"

Prayer After Communion   *BCW*, p. 76, no. 1

". . . Send us out in the power of your Spirit
[to proclaim the gospel for the salvation of humankind,
to work for the shelter, nurture, and spiritual
fellowship of the children of God;
to live a life shaped by the sacraments
inspired by the faithful maintenance of divine worship.
Lead us in the preservation of the truth, the promotion
of social righteousness, and the exhibition of the
Kingdom of Heaven to the world,
so that] we live and work for your praise and glory,
and for the sake of Jesus Christ our Lord."

Charge and Blessing   *BCW,* p. 78, no. 2

"[People of God, Church of Jesus Christ, you are called to . . .
insert one or more phrases of the great ends . . .]
Go in peace to love and serve the Lord."

Complete Orders of Worship

The following pages contain reproducible orders of worship that recall each of the six Great Ends. These are presented in both Service for the Lord's Day and Evening Prayer formats. Resource abbreviations, when they appear, refer to BOC, *The Book of Confessions;* PH (*The Presbyterian Hymnal*, 1990); PS (*The Psalter*, 1993); and BCW (*Book of Common Worship*, 1993). The larger liturgies might find their use in Lord's Day worship in local congregations, at festivals, at area church gatherings, in ecumenical settings, and at presbytery or synod meetings. The Order for Evening Prayer is appropriate for use in Bible study groups, men's and women's fellowship groups, support groups, retreats, session meetings, board of deacons meetings, and/or home use. Finally, an order of worship that uses the now familiar form of "Lessons and Hymns" is offered for special occasions in the life of a congregation or for other gatherings. These hymns and spiritual songs suggest a range of musical styles from which congregations can draw to reflect the rich musical heritage of the church.

Conclusion

It is important to remember that no matter how these resources are used, they are only one means to the greatest end: the worship of the Triune God. These ideas, and indeed the themes around which they are created, have value to us only insofar as they remind us of our vocation as the children of God and of our calling as the Church of Jesus Christ. While the individual components of the six Great Ends can be highlighted in isolation, it is only when all six are seen together that they can best offer a sense of balance to our corporate identity and our vision for ministry. The proclamation of the gospel without the attention to social righteousness can lead to empty rhetoric. Likewise, the preservation of the Truth or the offering of shelter and nurture without attention to acceptable worship (*Heb. 12:28—13:2*) can result in a form of benign humanism or self-righteousness. In liturgy, as in all of Christian life, it is in the blending of faith and action, Word and witness, that Christ is made known.

Order for Evening Prayer

Recalling the
"Proclamation of the Gospel for the Salvation of Humankind"

OPENING SENTENCES

Jesus Christ is the light of the world,
The light no darkness can overcome.
Stay with us Lord, for it is evening
and the day is almost over.
Let your light scatter the darkness
and illumine your church.

HYMN 546   "The Day Thou Gavest, Lord, Is Ended"

PSALM 8   PS 5

Silence for Reflection

PSALM PRAYER   *BCW*, p. 618

SCRIPTURE READING   *Romans 8:18–25*
The Word of the Lord.   **Thanks be to God.**

Silence for Reflection

HYMN 327   "O Word of God Incarnate"

PRAYERS OF THANKSGIVING AND INTERCESSION
                                            BCW, p. 519, no. 6

THE LORD'S PRAYER

HYMN 357   "O Master, Let Me Walk with Thee"

DISMISSAL

May the grace of the Lord Jesus Christ be with us all.
Amen.
Bless the Lord.
The Lord's name be praised.

Worship Service for
The Great Ends of the Church

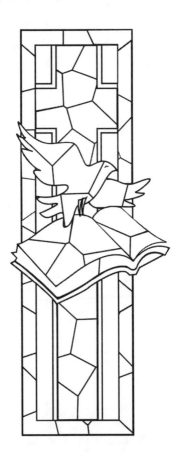

First Great End

*"Proclamation of the Gospel for the
Salvation of Humankind"*

Order of Worship

Recalling the
"Proclamation of the Gospel for the Salvation of Humankind" One of the Six Great Ends of the Church

. . . the Gospel is properly called glad and joyous news . . .
—Second Helvetic Confession (*BOC,* 5.089)

GATHERING

ENTRANCE SONG   "Though I May Speak with Bravest Fire"   PH 335

OPENING SENTENCES
> Long ago, God spoke to our ancestors
> in many and various ways by the prophets
> **But in these last days God has spoken to us by a Son.**
> *Hebrews 1:1–2b*

OPENING PRAYER   *BCW,* p. 201, no. 3

HYMN 220   "All People That on Earth Do Dwell"

CALL TO CONFESSION

PRAYER OF CONFESSION   *BCW,* p. 89, no. 6

DECLARATION OF FORGIVENESS

THE PEACE

THE WORD

> Indeed, God did not send the Son into the world to condemn
> the world,
> **but in order that the world might be saved through him.**
> *John 3:17*

PRAYER FOR ILLUMINATION

FIRST READING   *Isaiah 43:1–13*
> The Word of the Lord.   **Thanks be to God.**

PSALM 29   PS 26

SECOND READING   *1 John 4:7–21*
    The Word of the Lord.   **Thanks be to God.**

RESPONSE "Amen"   PH 299

GOSPEL READING   *John 15:18–27*
    The Word of the Lord.   **Thanks be to God.**

SERMON

AFFIRMATION OF FAITH

PRAYERS OF THE PEOPLE

THE EUCHARIST

For as often as you eat this bread and drink the cup,
You proclaim the Lord's death until he comes.
1 Corinthians 11:26

OFFERING

INVITATION TO THE LORD'S TABLE

GREAT THANKSGIVING

COMMUNION OF THE PEOPLE

PRAYER AFTER COMMUNION

SENDING

You will receive power when the Holy Spirit has come upon
you; **and you will be my witnesses in Jerusalem, in all
Judea and Samaria, and to the ends of the earth.** *Acts 1:8*

HYMN 411   "Arise, Your Light Is Come!"

CHARGE AND BLESSING

Order for Evening Prayer

Recalling the
"Shelter, Nurture, and Spiritual Fellowship of the Children of God"

OPENING SENTENCES   *BCW*, p. 509, no. 3

HYMN 281   "Guide Me, O Thou Great Jehovah"

PSALM 30   PH 181

Silence for Reflection

PSALM PRAYER   *BCW*, p. 643

SCRIPTURE READING   *Philippians 1:2–11*
    The Word of the Lord.   **Thanks be to God.**

Silence for Reflection

PRAYERS OF THANKSGIVING AND INTERCESSION   *BCW*, p. 519, no. 6

THE LORD'S PRAYER   PH 589

CANTICLE OF MARY   PH 600

HYMN 354   "Guide My Feet"

DISMISSAL
    May the grace of the Lord Jesus Christ be with us all.
    Amen.
    Bless the Lord.
    The Lord's name be praised.

Worship Service for
The Great Ends of the Church

Second Great End

*"Shelter, Nurture, and Spiritual Fellowship
of the Children of God"*

Order of Worship

Recalling the
"Shelter, Nurture, and Spiritual Fellowship of the Children of God" One of the Six Great Ends of the Church

I believe that, from the beginning to the end of the world, and
from among the whole human race, the Son of God . . . gathers,
protects, and preserves . . . , in the unity of the true faith,
a congregation chosen for eternal life. Moreover, I believe that I
am and forever will remain a living member of it.

—The Heidelberg Catechism (*BOC,* 4.054)

GATHERING

ENTRANCE SONG   PS 97

OPENING SENTENCES
God is our refuge and strength,
a very present help in trouble.
The LORD of hosts is with us,
the God of Jacob is our refuge.
Psalm 46:1, 7

OPENING PRAYER   *BCW*, p. 714

HYMN 461   "God Is Here!"

CALL TO CONFESSION

PRAYER OF CONFESSION   *BCW*, p. 55, no. 3

DECLARATION OF FORGIVENESS

THE PEACE

THE WORD

Do not be conformed to this world,
but be transformed by the renewing of your minds,
**so that you may discern what is the good will of
God—what is good and acceptable and perfect.**
Romans 12:2

PRAYER FOR ILLUMINATION

FIRST READING   *Isaiah 42:1–9*
    The Word of the Lord.   **Thanks be to God.**

PSALM 63:1–8   PS 54

SECOND READING   *Ephesians 1:8–14*
    The Word of the Lord.   **Thanks be to God.**

RESPONSE "Gloria, Gloria"   PH 576

GOSPEL READING   *Mark 10:13–16*
    The Word of the Lord.   **Thanks be to God.**

SERMON

THE APOSTLES' CREED   PH, p. 14

PRAYERS OF THE PEOPLE

THE EUCHARIST

O taste and see that the LORD is good;
happy are those who take refuge in him.
Psalm 34:8

OFFERING

INVITATION TO THE LORD'S TABLE

GREAT THANKSGIVING

COMMUNION OF THE PEOPLE

PRAYER AFTER COMMUNION

SENDING

When we cry "Abba! Father!" it is that very Spirit bearing
witness with our spirit that we are children of God.
**And if children, then heirs, heirs of God and joint heirs
with Christ.**   *Romans 8:15–17*

HYMN 442   "The Church's One Foundation"

CHARGE AND BLESSING

Order for Evening Prayer

Recalling the
"Maintenance of Divine Worship"

OPENING PRAYER   *BCW,* p. 530, no. 1

HYMN 464   "Joyful, Joyful, We Adore Thee"

PSALM 96   PH 217

Silence for Reflection

PSALM PRAYER   *BCW*, p. 720

SCRIPTURE READING   *Colossians 3:1–4, (5–11), 12–17*
   The Word of the Lord.   **Thanks be to God.**

Silence for Reflection

PRAYERS OF THANKSGIVING AND INTERCESSION   *BCW*, p. 517, no. 1

THE LORD'S PRAYER

HYMN 545   "Now, on Land and Sea Descending"

DISMISSAL
   May the grace of the Lord Jesus Christ be with us all.
   Amen.
   Bless the Lord.
   The Lord's name be praised.

Worship Service for
The Great Ends of the Church

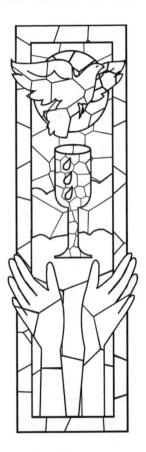

Third Great End

"Maintenance of Divine Worship"

Order of Worship

Recalling the
"Maintenance of Divine Worship"
One of the Six Great Ends of the Church

The church gathers to praise God, to hear God's word for humankind, to baptize and to join in the Lord's Supper, to pray for and to present the world to God in worship, to enjoy fellowship, to receive instruction, strength and comfort, to order and organize its own corporate life, to be tested, renewed, and reformed, and to speak and act in the world's affairs as may be appropriate to the needs of the times.

—Confession of 1967 (*BOC,* 9.36)

GATHERING

ENTRANCE SONG   "Heleluyan: Alleluia"   PH 595

OPENING SENTENCES
> This is the day that the Lord has made.
> **Let us rejoice and be glad in it!**
> *Psalm 118:24*

OPENING PRAYER

> Holy God, you call us to worship and by your Spirit prompt prayers and praise. Keep us from saying words or singing hymns with ritual disinterest. Fill us with such wonder that we may worship you, grateful for the mystery of your unfailing love for us, through Jesus Christ our Lord.
> **Amen.**

HYMN 253   "I'll Praise My Maker While I've Breath"

CALL TO CONFESSION

PRAYER OF CONFESSION   *BCW*, p. 180

DECLARATION OF FORGIVENESS

THE PEACE

HYMN 264   "When in Our Music God Is Glorified"

THE WORD

PRAYER FOR ILLUMINATION

FIRST READING   *Isaiah 52:7–10*
    The Word of the Lord.   **Thanks be to God.**

PSALM 150   PH 258

SECOND READING   *Romans 10:5–17*
    The Word of the Lord.   **Thanks be to God.**

HYMN 40   "Joy to the World! The Lord Is Come"

GOSPEL READING   *John 4:5–24*
    The Word of the Lord.   **Thanks be to God.**

SERMON

REAFFIRMATION OF BAPTISMAL VOWS   *BCW*, pp. 464–488

HYMN 492   "Baptized in Water"

PRAYERS OF THE PEOPLE

THE EUCHARIST

OFFERING

HYMN 514   "Let Us Talents and Tongues Employ"

INVITATION TO THE LORD'S TABLE

GREAT THANKSGIVING

COMMUNION OF THE PEOPLE

DISTRIBUTION HYMN 507   "I Come with Joy to Meet My Lord"

PRAYER AFTER COMMUNION

SENDING

HYMN 146   "Rejoice, Ye Pure in Heart"

CHARGE AND BLESSING

Order for Evening Prayer

Recalling the
"Preservation of the Truth"

OPENING SENTENCES

The people who walked in darkness have seen a great light.
**The light shines in the darkness and the darkness cannot
overcome it.**
Those who dwell in the land of deep darkness, on them has
light dawned.
**We have beheld his glory, glory as of the only Son of
the Father.**
In him was life, and the life was the light of all people.

HYMN 544   "Day Is Done"

PSALM 25   PS 23

Silence for Reflection

PSALM PRAYER   *BCW,* p. 637

SCRIPTURE READING   *1 John 4:1–6*
The Word of the Lord.   **Thanks be to God.**

Silence for Reflection

PRAYERS OF THANKSGIVING AND INTERCESSION   *BCW,* p. 518, no. 3

THE LORD'S PRAYER

CANTICLE OF MARY   PH 600

HYMN 331   "Thanks to God Whose Word Was Written"

DISMISSAL

May the grace of the Lord Jesus Christ be with us all.
Amen.
Bless the Lord.
The Lord's name be praised.

Worship Service for
The Great Ends of the Church

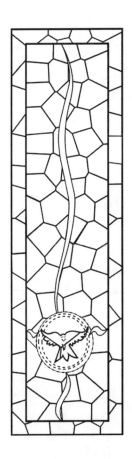

Fourth Great End

❦

"Preservation of the Truth"

❦

Order of Worship

Recalling the
"Preservation of the Truth"
One of the Six Great Ends of the Church

As Jesus Christ is God's assurance of the forgiveness of all our sins, so in the same way and with the same seriousness he is also God's mighty claim upon our whole life. Through him befalls us a joyful deliverance from the godless fetters of this world for a free, grateful service to his creatures.

—Theological Declaration of Barmen (*BOC*, 8.14)

GATHERING

OPENING SENTENCES

Jesus said:
"I am the way, and the truth, and the life.
No one comes to the Father except through me."
John 14:6

Praise the Lord.
The Lord's name be praised.

PRAYER OF THE DAY   *BCW*, p. 51, no. 4

HYMN 477   "Ye Servants of God, Your Master Proclaim"

PRAYER OF CONFESSION   *BCW*, p. 349

DECLARATION OF FORGIVENESS

THE PEACE

THE WORD

Jesus said:
"Do not let your hearts be troubled. Believe in God,
believe also in me."   *John 14:1*

PRAYER FOR ILLUMINATION

FIRST READING   *Deuteronomy 11:1–7, 18–21*
The Word of the Lord.   **Thanks be to God.**

PSALM 27   PH 179

SECOND READING   *Ephesians 4:17—5:2*
    The Word of the Lord.   **Thanks be to God.**

GOSPEL READING   *John 15:1–11*
    The Word of the Lord.   **Thanks be to God.**

SERMON

HYMN 314   "Like the Murmur of the Dove's Song"

AFFIRMATION OF FAITH

PRAYERS OF THE PEOPLE

THE EUCHARIST

    Jesus said:
    **"I am the vine, you are the branches. . . . Apart from me
    you can do nothing."**   *John 15:5*

OFFERTORY

INVITATION TO THE LORD'S TABLE

GREAT THANKSGIVING

COMMUNION OF THE PEOPLE

DISTRIBUTION HYMN 518   "Sheaves of Summer"

PRAYER AFTER COMMUNION

THE SENDING

    Jesus said:

    **"Go, therefore, and make disciples of all nations,
    baptizing them in the name of the Father and of the Son
    and of the Holy Spirit, and teaching them to obey every
    thing that I have commanded you."** *Matthew 28:19–20*

HYMN 429   "Lord, You Give the Great Commission"

CHARGE AND BLESSING

Order for Evening Prayer

Recalling the
"Promotion of Social Righteousness"

OPENING SENTENCES

For once you were darkness, but now in the LORD you are
light. Live as children of light.   *Ephesians 5:8*

**Because the LORD has anointed me; he has sent me . . . to
proclaim liberty to the captives, and release to the
prisoners; to proclaim the year of the LORD's favor. . . .
The LORD will cause righteousness and praise to spring up
before all the nations.**   *Isaiah 61:1b–2a, 11b*

HYMN 552   "Give Thanks, O Christian People"

PSALM 139   PS 142–143

Silence for Reflection

PSALM PRAYER   *BCW*, p. 771

SCRIPTURE READING   *Luke 14:7–14*
The Word of the Lord.   **Thanks be to God.**

Silence for Reflection

PRAYERS OF THANKSGIVING AND INTERCESSION   *BCW*, p. 518, no. 4

THE LORD'S PRAYER

HYMN 435   "We All Are One in Mission"

DISMISSAL

May the grace of the Lord Jesus Christ be with us all.
Amen.
Bless the Lord.
The Lord's name be praised.

Worship Service for
The Great Ends of the Church

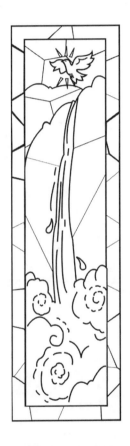

Fifth Great End

"Promotion of Social Righteousness"

Order of Worship

Recalling the
"Promotion of Social Righteousness"
One of the Six Great Ends of the Church

In a broken and fearful world, the Spirit gives us courage to pray
without ceasing, to witness among all peoples to Christ as Lord
and Savior, to unmask idolatries in Church and culture, to hear
the voices of people long silenced, and to work with others for
justice, freedom, and peace.   —A Brief Statement of Faith

THE GATHERING

CALL TO WORSHIP
  God has told you, O mortal, what is good. And what does the
  LORD require of you?
  To do justice, and love kindness, and to walk humbly with GOD.
                                                    Micah 6:8b

OPENING PRAYER   *BCW*, p. 819, no. 68

HYMN 427   "Lord, Whose Love Through Humble Service"

CALL TO CONFESSION

PRAYER OF CONFESSION   *BCW*, p. 54, no. 4
  "Lord, Have Mercy Upon Us"   PH 572

DECLARATION OF FORGIVENESS
  "Arise, Your Light Is Come"   PH 411

THE PEACE

THE WORD

Let justice roll down like waters, and righteousness like an
everflowing stream.   *Amos 5:24*

Happy are those who observe justice, who do
righteousness at all times.   *Psalm 106:2–3*

FIRST READING   *Micah 6:6–8*
  The Word of the Lord.   **Thanks be to God.**

PSALM 51   PS 48

SECOND READING   *James 1:22–27*
    The Word of the Lord.   **Thanks be to God.**

GOSPEL READING   *Matthew 5:1–16*
    The Word of the Lord.   **Thanks be to God.**

HYMN 407   "Cuando el Pobre / When a Poor One"

SERMON

HYMN 436   "We Are Your People, Lord, by Your Grace"

PRAYERS OF THE PEOPLE

THE EUCHARIST

See, the home of God is among mortals. . . . Mourning and crying
and pain will be no more. . . .
See, I am making all things new.   *Revelation 21:3a–5*

OFFERING HYMN 422   "God, Whose Giving Knows No Ending"

INVITATION TO THE LORD'S TABLE

GREAT THANKSGIVING

COMMUNION OF THE PEOPLE

DISTRIBUTION HYMN 367   "Jesu, Jesu, Fill Us with Your Love"

PRAYER AFTER COMMUNION

SENDING

You shall love the Lord your God with all your heart, and
with all your soul, and with all your mind. This is the first
and greatest commandment.
**And a second is like it: you shall love your neighbor as
yourself.**   *Matthew 22:37, 39*

HYMN 432   "Canto de Esperanza / Song of Hope"

CHARGE AND BLESSING

Order for Evening Prayer

Recalling the
"Exhibition of the Kingdom of Heaven to the World"

OPENING SENTENCES

Day and night without ceasing they sing:
**"Holy, holy, holy, the Lord God the Almighty, who
was and is and is to come."** *Revelation 4:8b*

HYMN 138   "Holy, Holy, Holy! Lord God Almighty!"

PSALM 148   PS 155

Silence for Reflection

PSALM PRAYER   *BCW*, p. 781

SCRIPTURE READING   *Galatians 5:1, 13–25*
The Word of the Lord.   **Thanks be to God.**

Silence for Reflection

HYMN 332   "Live Into Hope"

GOSPEL READING   *Luke 18:15–17*
The Word of the Lord.   **Thanks be to God.**

Silence for Reflection

PRAYERS OF THANKSGIVING AND INTERCESSION   *BCW*, p. 519, no. 5

THE LORD'S PRAYER   PH 571

CANTICLE OF THE NEW JERUSALEM   PS 177

HYMN 388   "O Jesus, I Have Promised"

DISMISSAL

May the grace of the Lord Jesus Christ be with us all.
Amen.
Bless the Lord.
The Lord's name be praised.

Worship Service for
The Great Ends of the Church

Sixth Great End

❧

*"Exhibition of the Kingdom of Heaven
to the World"*

❧

Order of Worship

Recalling the
"Exhibition of the Kingdom of Heaven to the World"
One of the Six Great Ends of the Church

Already God's reign is present as a ferment in this world, stirring hope in men and women and preparing the world to receive its ultimate judgment and redemption. With an urgency born of this hope, the church applies itself to present tasks and strives for a better world. It does not identify limited progress with the kingdom of God on earth, nor does it despair in the face of disappointment and defeat. In steadfast hope, the church looks beyond all partial achievement to the final triumph of God.

—Confession of 1967 (*BOC*, 9.54–55)

GATHERING

OPENING SENTENCES

> The LORD is a great God who says,
> **"I am the Alpha and the Omega,
> the first and the last,
> the beginning and the end."** *Revelation 22:13*

> Let us worship God.

HYMN 229 (st. 1–2)   "From All That Dwell Below the Skies"

PRAYER OF CONFESSION   *BCW*, p. 334

DECLARATION OF FORGIVENESS

HYMN 229 (st. 3)

THE PEACE

THE WORD

> The time is fulfilled, and the kingdom of God has come near;
> **repent, and believe the good news.** *Mark 1:14*

FIRST READING   *Jeremiah 31:31–34*
> The Word of the Lord.   **Thanks be to God.**

PSALM 36:5–10   PS 34

SECOND READING   *Revelation 3:14b–22*
    The Word of the Lord.   **Thanks be to God.**

RESPONSE "Alleluia"   PH 595

GOSPEL READING   *Matthew 13:24–33*
    The Word of the Lord.   **Thanks be to God.**

SERMON

HYMN 1   "Come, Thou Long-Expected Jesus"

AFFIRMATION OF FAITH   The Great Ends of the Church

PRAYERS OF THE PEOPLE

HYMN RESPONSE 599   "Jesus Remember Me"

THE EUCHARIST

Then people will come from east and west, from north and south
and will eat in the kingdom of God.   *Luke 13:29*

OFFERING HYMN 358   "Help Us Accept Each Other"

INVITATION TO THE LORD'S TABLE

GREAT THANKSGIVING

COMMUNION OF THE PEOPLE

DISTRIBUTION HYMN 300   "Down to Earth as a Dove"

SENDING

"It is not for you to know the times or periods
that the Father has set by his own authority.
**But you will receive power when the Holy Spirit
has come upon you; and you will be my witnesses."**
                                                  Acts 1:7–8

HYMN 447   "Lead On, O King Eternal"

CHARGE AND BLESSING   *BCW*, p. 160, no. 6, p. 161, no. 4

A Festival of Lessons and Hymns

Recalling the
Six Great Ends of the Church

CALL TO WORSHIP

The earth is the Lord's and all that is in it.
The world, and those who live in it;
Now, this is what the Lord said, "I have called you by
name, you are mine."
**Come, let us sing to the Lord. Let us make a joyful noise to
the rock of our salvation!**
Now, this is what the Savior said, "I am the way and the truth
and the life."
O sing to the Lord a new song; sing to the Lord, all the earth.
Now, by the power of the Holy Spirit, we shall be Christ's
witnesses . . . to all the ends of the earth.

HYMN 229   "From All That Dwell Below the Skies"

The Proclamation of the Gospel for
the Salvation of Humankind

FIRST READING   *Genesis 12:1–2*

HYMN 488   "The God of Abraham Praise"

SECOND READING   *Matthew 28:16–20*

HYMN 429   "Lord, You Give the Great Commission"

The Shelter, Nurture, and Spiritual Fellowship
of the Children of God

THIRD READING   *Ezekiel 34:11–16*

HYMN 387   "Savior, Like a Shepherd Lead Us"

FOURTH READING   *Ephesians 2:17–22*

HYMN 296   "Camina Pueblo de Dios / Walk On, O People Of God"